Adult Meth

T0081758

Beginner Level

By Wesley Schaum

Teacher Consultants: Alfred Cahn, Joan Cupp, Sue Pennington

Schaum's Pathway to Musicianship

The *Schaum Making Music Piano Library* integrates method, theory, technic and note reading with appealing materials for recital and repertoire. Schaum's well-proven motivational philosophy and sound pedagogy are widely recognized.

FOREWORD

This method is tailored for <u>the older beginner</u> – adult or teenager. It may also be used for mature students of a younger age.

The progress here is <u>much more gradual than other adult methods</u>. This allows the student to be entirely comfortable with the learning steps. The rate of progress is flexible; work in this book can be leisurely or fast paced, depending upon the individual pupil and preference of the teacher.

No simplified piano music is used. The musical excerpts are themes from symphonies, operas, ballets, concertos, oratorios, chamber music, vocal and choral literature. Also included are folk songs from many ethnic groups. Emphasis is placed on music appreciation stories and pictures of the composers and musical instruments.

A <u>minimum of finger numbers</u> are used. Various changed and extended hand positions are used to avoid becoming locked into a rigid five-finger position. Simple transposing is featured. Broken chords are used instead of blocked chords for ease of performance at this level.

INDEX

Exclusively Distributed By

HAL•LEONARD®
CORPORATION

7777 W. BLUEMOUND RD. P.O. BOX 13819 MILWAUKEE, WI 53213

ISBN-13: 978-1-936098-54-5

REFERENCE PAGE — also see Music Dictionary (page 47) and Index (page 48).

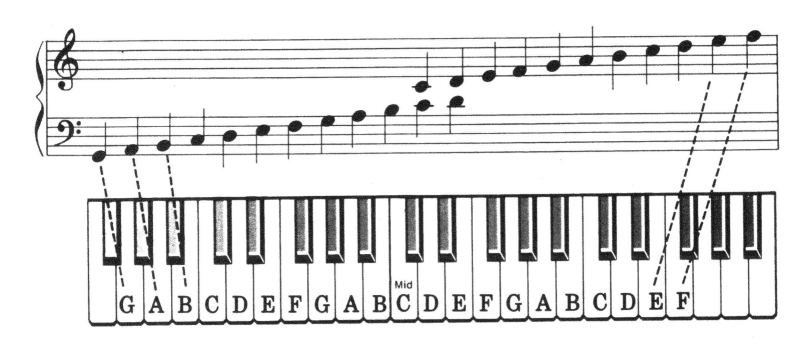

G A B C D E F G A B C Mid **D E F G A B C D E F**

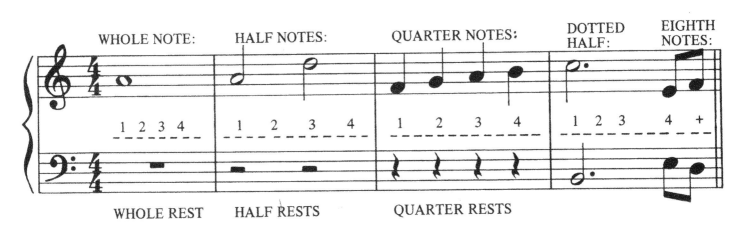

WHOLE NOTE: HALF NOTES: QUARTER NOTES: DOTTED HALF: EIGHTH NOTES:

1 2 3 4   1 2 3 4   1 2 3 4   1 2 3 4 +

WHOLE REST   HALF RESTS   QUARTER RESTS

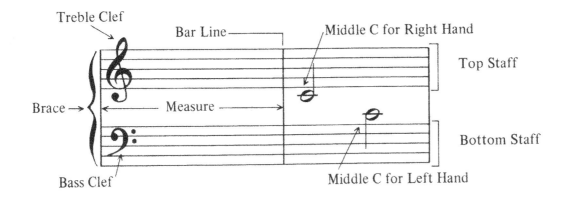

Treble Clef

Bar Line — Middle C for Right Hand

Top Staff

Brace → Measure

Bass Clef

Middle C for Left Hand

Bottom Staff

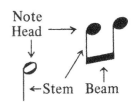

Note Head →

←Stem Beam

$\boldsymbol{f}$ = Loud (*forte*)

$\boldsymbol{p}$ = Soft (*piano*)

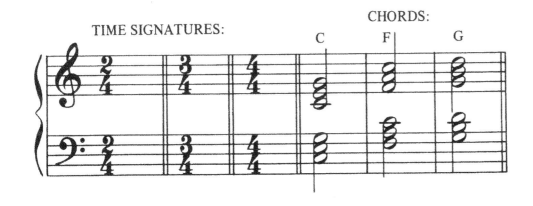

TIME SIGNATURES:

CHORDS:

C   F   G

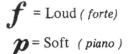

♯ = Sharp

♭ = Flat

♮ = Natural

Contents

4

Development and History of the Piano

The development of keyboard instruments with strings began in Italy prior to 1500. At the start of the 16th century, the **clavichord** had some of the elements of the modern piano: metal strings, a soundboard to amplify the sound, hammers to strike the strings, and dampers to stop the strings from ringing. The very soft, delicate tone of the clavichord was a disadvantage, but its simple mechanism was touch-sensitive, enabling performers to play expressively.

The **harpsichord** had a mechanism to pluck the strings. Although its keyboard was not touch-sensitive, its larger frame and winged shape, forerunner of the modern grand piano, gave it a bigger sound. For this reason, the harpsichord was widely used from the 1600's into the early 1800's and is still employed for authentic performances of music from these times. More sophisticated harpsichords had two keyboards and several sets of strings, which could be played alone or in combination to produce contrasts in loudness and tone quality.

The piano was developed because of a desire to combine the expressive touch-sensitivity of the clavichord with the larger sound of the harpsichord. In the 1700's, an Italian named Cristofori invented an improved hammer action and a stronger wing shaped case that held longer and thicker strings. Cristofori called his new instrument the **pianoforte**, which in Italian, literally means "soft-loud," because its touch-sensitive keyboard was able to produce both soft and loud sounds. As the pianoforte was refined it eventually overshadowed the harpsichord in popularity.

The strings of the clavichord, harpsichord, and pianoforte were attached to wooden frames. Although the later frames were reinforced with metal to make them stronger and more stable, these instruments did not stay in tune very well; most had to be tuned each time they were used, like a violin. The development of the cast iron piano frame in 1825 was significant for its improvement in tuning stability. Its great strength enabled the use of thicker strings under greater tension for better volume and quality of sound. American piano makers, Chickering and Steinway made important improvements to the cast iron frame.

From the mid 1800's into the early 1900's, there was brisk competition among numerous piano manufacturers in Europe and the United States. This stimulated development of the upright piano and many refinements in tone quality and touch-sensitivity which are common today. Between 1900 and 1930, the height of popularity of the piano, there were several hundred brands of pianos manufactured in 17 different states. Illinois, Massachusetts, and New York had the largest number of factories.

During that time, the player-piano (an automatic playing mechanism) became very popular, since radio and TV were non-existent, and the sound quality of cylinder and disk recordings was poor. Before the development of plastics in the 1940's, ivory was used to cover the white keys. "Tickling the ivories" was common slang for playing the piano.

Today, three sizes of upright pianos are made - spinet, console and studio - each progressively larger. The increased size contributes to a bigger sound and better tone quality, especially in the lower range. Grand pianos are also made in several sizes from the 5-foot "baby grand" to a 12-foot concert grand.

CLAVICHORD

HARPSICHORD

GRAND PIANO

Electronic and digital pianos, developed in the late 1980's, represent a new development in keyboard instruments. As a result, the traditional piano with strings and hammers is now called an "acoustic piano." Like the acoustic piano, which took many years to be developed, these electronic instruments are still being improved in the areas of sound quality and touch-sensitivity.

Music and Sports

To the casual viewer, professional athletes on TV make their sport seem deceptively simple. Most people, however, realize that to become skilled in basketball, swimming, tennis, skiing, etc. requires muscle development, study and tactics, lots of practice, and the supervision of a coach or trainer. Athletes are continually exercising with calisthenics, weights, conditioning machines, and other practice routines beyond actual participation in their sport.

Watching a professional pianist or other musician, likewise, makes a performance seem quite easy. The physical training and skills involved with playing an instrument are very much like those in sports but less obvious. When playing the piano, for example, the hands, feet, and body have subtle movements involving many small muscles that are not particularly noticeable. The coordination of ears, eyes, and fingers, although almost imperceptible, is as vital to success as the more obvious skills exhibited in tennis or basketball.

A concert pianist playing a full length recital needs the physical endurance of a front-line soccer player, the controlled strength of a champion gymnast, and the concentration of an expert golfer.

Both music and sports have these essentials to be learned:

- Terminology, rules and regulations
- Handling and maintenance of equipment
- Proper warm-ups
- Required strength and endurance
- Muscle control and coordination
- Strategy and tactics for success

In addition, the enjoyment of both music an sports is enhanced by a knowledge of the history, development, and of outstanding performers.

Posture and Seating Position

Sit up straight, not rigidly but comfortably, so that your shoulders are not hunched forward. It is preferable to sit on the front part of the bench or chair with very little of the thigh contacting the bench. This permits freedom of arm, leg and body movement, which becomes increasingly important as you progress.

The ideal seating height should position the body so that the underside of the forearms are nearly level with the keyboard. This will put the wrist and hand into place where a good hand position can be established. If necessary, use a chair instead of the bench, or add a cushion or thick book.

Hand Position

Fingers should be curved so that the tip of each finger, just behind the fingernail, contacts the piano key (except the thumb, of course). Grasping a tennis ball (or with a larger hand, a baseball/hardball) will give approximately the correct finger curvature. Long fingernails, unfortunately, will interfere. It is possible to play with longer fingernails, but the altered hand position impedes maximum leverage and limits control and strength.

Curving the fingers compensates for the difference in length between the thumb and other fingers and will enable the thumb to cross under the other fingers, used frequently in more advanced music.

Wrists, Arms and Elbows

The back of the hand should be almost flat (horizontal). A good test is to place a large coin or bottle cap on the back of the hands. The coin or cap should not slide off when the keys are played.

As with sports, efficiency of movement and conservation of physical energy are important aspects of piano playing. Wasted and unneeded movements make playing not only awkward but unnecessarily tiring. In the long run, these wasted movements will impede both dexterity and endurance.

The wrist should have relatively little vertical movement while playing. Constantly moving the wrist up and down, like a pump handle, is a common example of wasted movement.

Movement of the forearm and elbow should also be minimized. Exaggerated side-to-side elbow movement is not needed to achieve a good phrase release. This "elbow flapping" is another example of wasted movement and energy.

Basic Rhythm for Starting

Rhythm . . . . Timing of music regulated by a steady pulse or beat.

Note . . . . Oval shaped musical symbol.
The note **head** (round part) may be hollow or solid black.
It most often has a **stem** (short vertical line) attached.

Whole Note . . . . . Thick hollow note; the only note with no stem.
Named because it fills a *whole* measure.

Quarter Note . . . Solid black note with a stem.
Named because it is one *quarter* the duration of a whole note.

Bar Line . . . . Vertical line separating groups of notes into measures.

Measure . . . . Space, between bar lines, used to organize the rhythm of music.

Directions: Music notes for rhythm are read like a book, from left to right. Your teacher will help you to count and clap the rhythm to the notes below. The counting numbers are printed below the notes. At first, be sure to count aloud. Keep your counting very steady and even, with the same length of time for each number. Clap hands for each note. Hands should remain together for the entire duration of a *whole note*.

Steady, evenly-spaced counting is essential.
It will become the basic pulse for all rhythm as you advance in music study.

Directions: Play the rhythm written above using right hand thumb on middle-C and other C's on the keyboard. Count aloud as you play. Then do the same with left hand thumb. For extra work, play A, B, D, and E, using the rhythm written above.

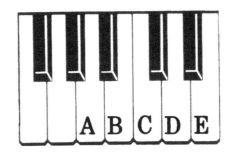

Teacher's Note: Time signatures are purposely omitted here. 4/4, along with other time signatures, will be explained later. The rhythms presented here are also used on pages 7, 8, 9 and 10.

Musical Alphabet

The musical alphabet uses only the letters A through G. These seven letters are repeated over and over as shown in the keyboard segment below.

The keyboard contains groups of 2 and 3 black keys. Notice that as the letters repeat, they fit with the same black key group. For example, "D" is always between the group of 2 black keys.

Up and Down at the Keyboard

Musical sounds become *higher* as you move to the *right* of the keyboard; they become *lower* as you move to the *left* at the keyboard.

As you move up, the musical alphabet goes *forward*; as you move down, the musical alphabet goes *backward*.

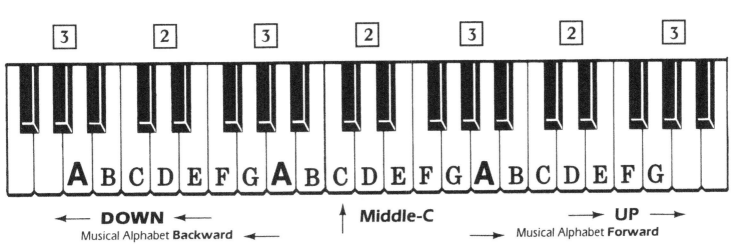

3-Letter Warm-Up for Right Hand

Directions: Place right hand thumb on Middle-C (see diagram above). Using one finger for each white key, play this 3-letter warm-up using the same rhythm as on the previous page. For extra practice, start on different C's (above or below middle-C)

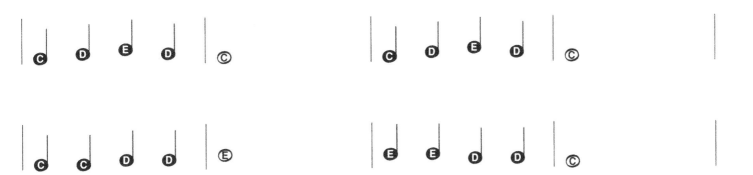

3-Letter Warm-Up for Left Hand

Directions: Place left hand thumb on Middle-C (see diagram above). Using one finger for each white key, play this 3-letter warm-up using the same rhythm as on the previous page. For extra practice, start on different C's (above or below middle-C)

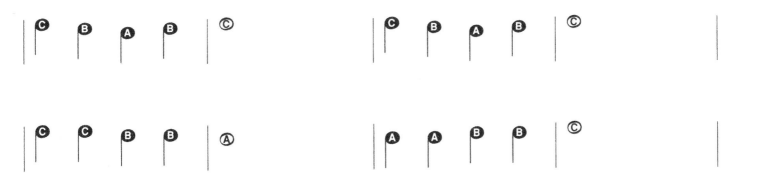

Schaum's **Theory Workbook, Primer Level** provides written work coordinated with this book to reinforce the learning elements.

Note Movement: Up, Down, or Repeat

Music notes may move UP or DOWN like stair steps, as shown below. Music notes are REPEATED when the notes remain on the *same level*. Your eye will be trained to recognize these note movements and coordinate them with finger movements at the keyboard. You can start training your ear by *listening* to the sound of these note movements.

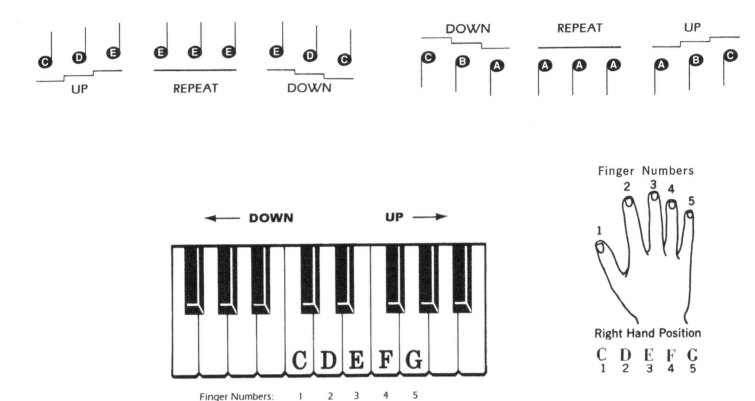

5-Letter Warm-Up for Right Hand

Directions: Place right hand thumb on Middle-C. Use one finger for each white key, following the finger number diagram above. Play this 5-letter warm-up using the same rhythm as on page 6. Counting numbers are printed between the lines of notes.

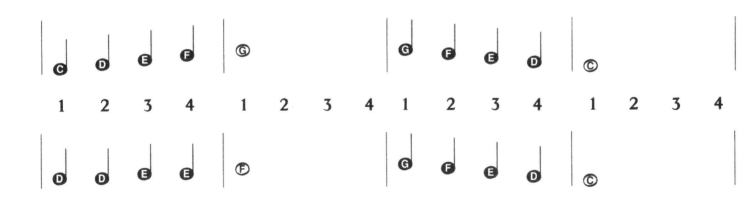

Eye Training Strategy

As with a typewriter or computer keyboard, when reading music, eyes should be trained to look mainly at the music *not at the hands or keyboard*. Although it will be a great temptation, try not to look down at your hands. Instead, you should develop your *sense of touch* so that fingers can "remember the feeling" of the different keys at the keyboard. As music becomes more advanced, the sense of touch should be developed to learn the feeling for different intervals and chords. The habit of keeping eyes on the music and finding the keys by your sense of touch will be invaluable. These same habits will promote fluent note reading of new music.

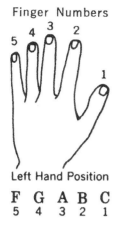

Finger Numbers

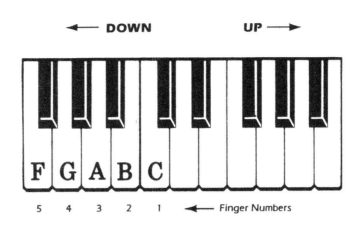

Left Hand Position

F G A B C
5 4 3 2 1

5-Letter Warm-Up for Left Hand

Directions: Place left hand thumb on Middle-C. Use one finger for each white key, following the finger number diagram above. Play this 5-letter warm-up using the same rhythm as on page 6. Counting numbers are printed between the lines of notes.

C B A G | F   F G A B | C

1 2 3 4 | 1 2 3 4 | 1 2 3 4 | 1 2 3 4

B B A A | G   F G A B | C

The Staff

Staff lines help you to see if notes move up, down, or are repeated. A note placed *between* any staff lines is said to be a "space note" or "in a space." A note with a staff line through its middle is said to be a "line note" or "on a line."

The staff has 5 lines with 4 spaces in between.

Be careful; a music note "on a line" is different than in penmanship, where "on a line," means just above the line.

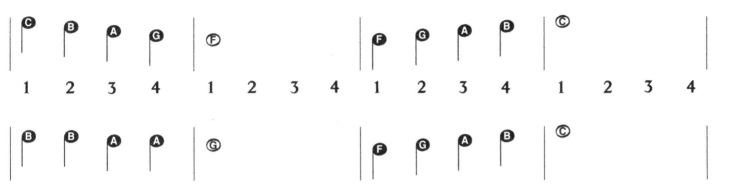

STAFF   SPACE NOTE   LINE NOTE

Treble Clef

The *top* staff is for notes in the *upper* part of the keyboard (for now, middle-C and above). It has an I.D. (identification) sign called a **treble clef**. The *right* hand usually plays notes written in the top staff.

Bass Clef

The *bottom* staff is for notes in the *lower* part of the keyboard (for now, middle-C and below). It has an I.D. (identification) sign called a **bass clef**. The *left* hand usually plays notes written in the bottom staff.

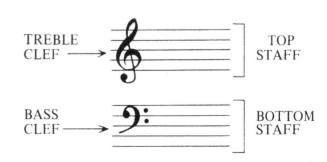

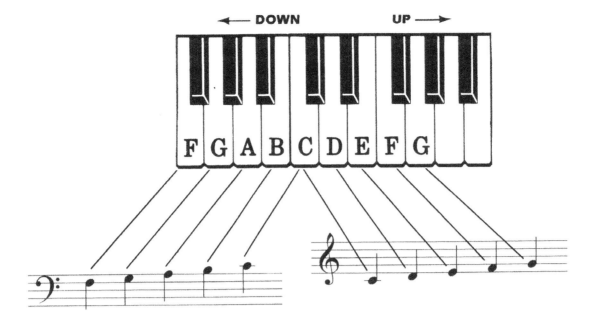

Legato (lah-GAH-toh) is an Italian word meaning smooth and connected with no interruption in sound. Notes at the piano are usually played legato (unless marked otherwise). You will need to develop the control in your fingers so one key is released just as the next key is depressed. The correct hand position helps you to play legato.

5-Note Warm-Up for Right Hand

Directions: Use hand position shown on page 8. Be sure to keep an even, steady beat as you play.
Try to play these notes *legato*. Counting numbers are printed between the staffs.

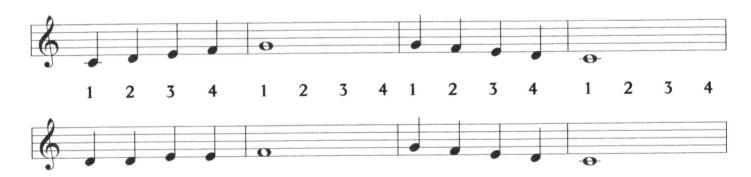

5-Note Warm-Up for Left Hand

Directions: Use hand position shown on page 9. Be sure to keep an even, steady beat as you play.
Try to play these notes *legato*. Counting numbers are printed between the staffs.

Teachers Note: The notes here are purposely the same as the warm-ups on pages 8 and 9.

A **brace** is the musical term for the bracket used to connect the treble staff and bass staff.

Notice the two different notes for Middle-C.

The middle-C in the *treble staff* is played with the right hand.

The middle-C in the *bass staff* is for the left hand.

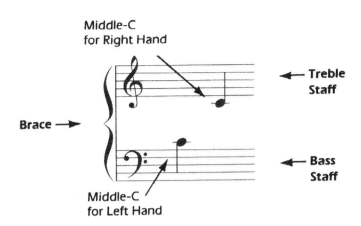

Keeping in Step

Directions: In this music, left and right hands play alternately. Notes in the *bottom* staff are for the left hand. *Top* staff notes are for the right hand. The small numbers between the staffs are **finger numbers**. These show what finger is to be used in each hand. (Use the right hand position shown on page 8 and the left hand position shown on page 9.)

The rhythm here is different from the previous pages. The counting numbers are the large numbers printed between the staffs. As a warm-up, count and clap the rhythm for the entire piece.

Practice Strategy

Always keep a written record of your lesson assignment. This will serve as your practice guide and objective each week. More important than the amount of time, is the *quality* **of your practice**. A surprising amount can be accomplished when full attention is focused on the practice objectives, even for a short period of 10 to 15 minutes. Obviously, this takes self-discipline, but also setting aside a "quiet time," free from interruptions. The time you spend at the piano will be much more productive when sounds from TV, stereo, etc. are minimized or eliminated. Family pets, children and visitors should be out of sight, and if possible, out of hearing range. Avoid doing two things at once such as cooking supper while practicing. Phones should not be answered during the time you practice either. The fewer distractions the better. If you have an electronic piano, headphones are often ideal for practice.

Regular practice is a simple but crucial element for success. As in sports, there is a substantial amount of muscular control and coordination which must be developed by practice. Try not to let more than one day go by without some practice – even if it's just ten or fifteen minutes. Although spending a whole hour at the piano is wonderful, a shorter time is easier to fit into a busy schedule. Regularity will be rewarded.

Suggested practice record books:

Lesson Assignment Book (#4013) or *Progressive Practice Plans (#4015)*, both published by Schaum Publications, Inc.

Intervals: 2nds and 3rds

An *interval* is the distance in sound between one note and another.

The *interval number* is the same as the number of *alphabet letters* that it includes.

It is also the same as the number of white keys involved.

> A to B is a *2nd*, because the distance in sound is 2 alphabet letters (A-B).
> B to C is also a *2nd*, because the distance is again 2 alphabet letters (B-C).
>
> A to C is a *3rd*, because the distance in sound is 3 alphabet letters (A-B-C).
> C to E is also a *3rd*, because the distance is again 3 alphabet letters (C-D-E).

Intervals between other letters are counted the same way.

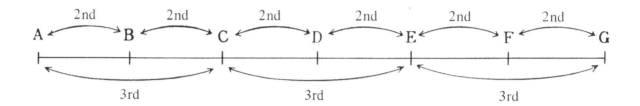

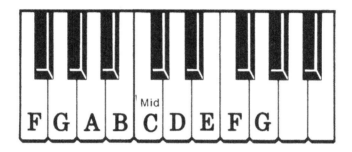

Seconds and Thirds

Directions: This piece uses intervals of 2nds and 3rds, up and down, along with a few repeated notes. If necessary, look back at page 8 for up, down, and repeat. Try to distinguish between the 2nds and 3rds *with your eyes* as you play. Your eyes recognize the interval from the notes and relay to the fingers the distance to reach.

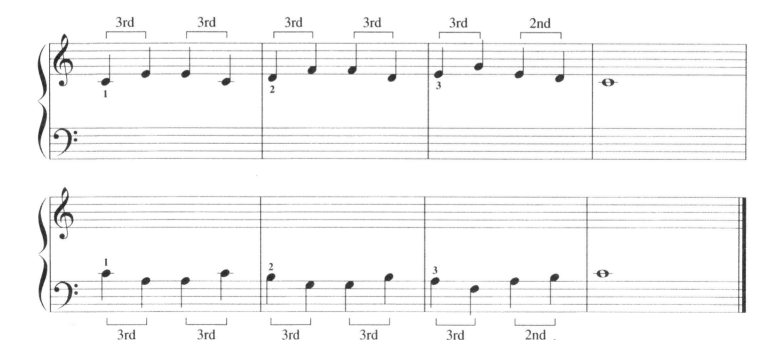

4 Time Signature

4 — UPPER number tells the number of *counts* or *beats* in each measure (see page 6).

4 — LOWER number tells the kind of note that gets one count.
In this case, the quarter note gets one count.

Half Note   Hollow note with a **stem** (short, vertical line). The stem may go up or down, depending on the position of the note in the staff.
Named because it is one *half* the duration of a whole note.
Gets <u>TWO</u> Counting Numbers or beats.

Quarter Note   Solid black note with a stem.
Named because it is one *quarter* the duration of a whole note.
Gets <u>ONE</u> Counting Number or beat.

Preparatory: Count and clap the rhythm to the notes below. The counting numbers are printed between the staffs. At first, be sure to count aloud. Keep your counting very steady and even, with the same length of time for each number. Clap hands for each note. Hands should remain together for the entire duration of a half note.

Theme from "Surprise Symphony" (Haydn)

Directions: Notes in the *top* staff are for the right hand. *Bottom* staff notes are for the left hand.
The small numbers printed close to a note are finger numbers.

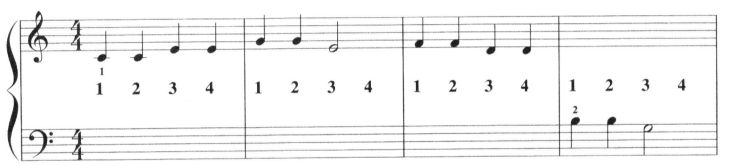

Franz Joseph Haydn (HIGH-den) • 1732-1809 • Austria

Haydn is considered the father of orchestral music, particularly the symphony, which was developed at that time. His style is happy, light and cheerful.

Much of Haydn's music was written during the 25 years he worked as court conductor for Count Esterhazy, a wealthy nobleman. Haydn wrote many string quartets, operas, oratorios, piano sonatas, and 104 symphonies. (See page 27 for description of the symphony.)

Symphony No. 94, the "Surprise Symphony," received its nickname because of a sudden loud chord following a soft melody. It is said that Haydn wrote this loud chord to awaken those in the audience who had become sleepy.

Dynamic Marks: f and p

Symbols and words are used in music to tell the performer where to play loud, soft and various shades in between. These are called *dynamic marks*, or sometimes, *expression marks*. Italian words and their abbreviations are often used. Because early music writing began in Italy, Italian has become the international language commonly used by composers.

On the piano, with its touch-sensitive keyboard, loud and soft are controlled by the weight and strength used in the fingers and hands when playing. Obviously, a heavy, strong touch will produce a loud sound. Concert pianists also develop their arms, shoulders and torso to help control dynamic levels.

At first, only two dynamic marks will be used. Try to play each finger *equally* loud (or soft). It is very important that you also LISTEN as you play and train your ear to recognize different dynamic levels.

f — Abbreviation of **forte** (FOHR-tay), an Italian word meaning loud or strong.

p — Abbreviation of **piano** (pee-YAH-noh), an Italian word meaning soft.

Theme from "Csardas (Bartok)

Directions: The rhythm in this piece is purposely the same as in the Haydn theme on page 13. For review or as a warm-up, count and clap the rhythm to the notes below. Arrows point out places where hands alternate. Your eye must become watchful for these hand changes.

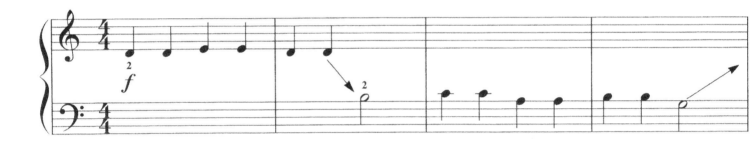

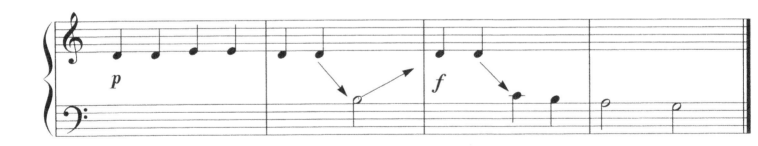

Bela Bartok (BAR-tokh) • 1881-1945 • Hungary

Bartok is remembered for his extensive efforts to record and preserve the folk music of his native country. Beginning in 1906 he made annual trips carrying Edison cylinder recording equipment into numerous villages, collecting over 6000 songs.

Bartok's compositions blended his native folk music with his own imaginative ideas. He wrote many works for piano from miniature student pieces to concertos. He also composed operas and music for orchestra, choir, solo voice and chamber groups.

A **csardas** (CHAR-dahsh) is a Hungarian national dance with contrasting slow and fast sections.

Eye Training: Reading Intervals Between Staffs

Fluent music reading depends upon training the eye to recognize different intervals between notes. If necessary, review up, down and repeat (page 8) and intervals (page 12). Extra care is needed when reading notes that move from one staff to another. The line below shows 2nds and 3rds between staffs. Notice that these intervals move both up and down. As a preparatory, play the line below five times per day. For extra practice, recite the letter names aloud as you play.

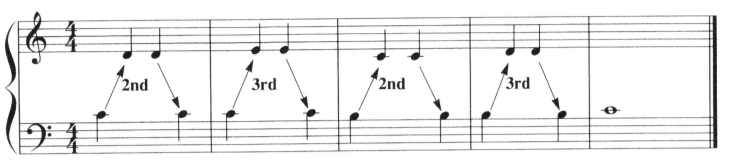

Yankee Doodle (American Folk Tune)

Directions: The intervals in this piece are found in the preparatory line above.
As a warm-up, count and clap the rhythm to the notes below. The arrows show intervals of 2nds and 3rds between staffs.

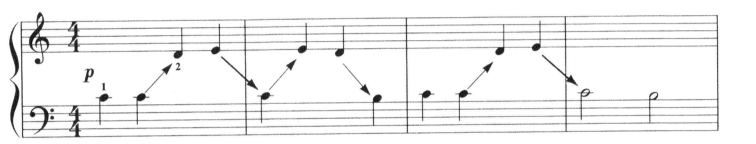

The tune, *Yankee Doodle*, probably originated in England in the middle 1700's. However, it became popular during the American Revolutionary War (1775-1783) and for this reason is generally considered an American folk tune. It was common for marching musicians playing fifes and drums to accompany foot-soldiers of the time. Marching music was an important morale booster. The **fife** was also used to signal commands between infantry units. The fife is a small wooden instrument shaped like a flute but with a higher, shrill sound. Active fife and drum marching groups are still found mainly in the New England states.

Folk music reflects local life, times and traditions, especially in rural areas. There is no known composer and usually the song has been passed from one generation to another without written music, resulting in differences in both melody and words.

3/4 Time Signature

3 — THREE *counts* or *beats* in each measure (see page 6).

4 — QUARTER note gets ONE count.

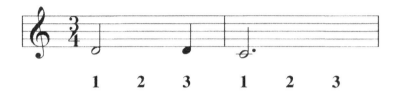

Dotted Half Note Half Note with a dot added on the *right side*. It gets <u>THREE</u> Counting Numbers. (Also see footnote.)

1   2   3   1   2   3

Preparatory: Count and clap the rhythm to the notes below. The counting numbers are printed between the staffs. Keep your counting very steady and even. Clap hands for each note. Hands should remain together for the entire duration of all *half notes* and *dotted half notes*.

Jesu, Joy of Man's Desiring (Bach)

Directions: The starting finger numbers are printed smaller. If necessary, add counting numbers to the second line of music.

Johann Sebastian Bach (BAHKH) • 1685-1750 • Germany

Bach, one of the world's most famous composers, came from a large family of musicians and had twenty children of his own, many of whom became musicians. His works include choral, orchestral, organ, and keyboard music. Bach's keyboard music was written for the harpsichord and clavichord (see page 4) because the recently developed piano was not widely used.

Bach wrote hundreds of compositions during his lifetime including many sacred and secular cantatas. A **cantata** (cahn-TAH-tah) is a work for orchestra, solo voices, and chorus, often telling a story. This melody is from a chorale section of Cantata No. 147, written in 1723.

Note: A dot added on the right side of a note increases the value of that note by half. In 4/4 and 3/4 time, a half note gets two counts; the dot adds one extra count for a total of three. Other notes may also have dots to extend their duration.

New Treble Note: A
The position of the note A is shown on the keyboard diagram below.

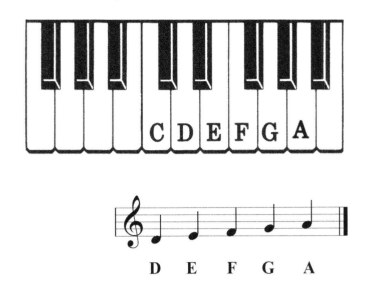

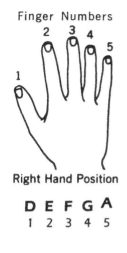

Finger Numbers

Right Hand Position

D E F G A
1 2 3 4 5

Morning from "Peer Gynt Suite" (Grieg)

Directions: A new hand position is used in the right hand. See the fingering diagram above. The thumb now will play the note D. The 5th finger is used to play the new note A. Arrows are used to show where hands alternate. If helpful, add brackets above other 3rd intervals like the samples below.

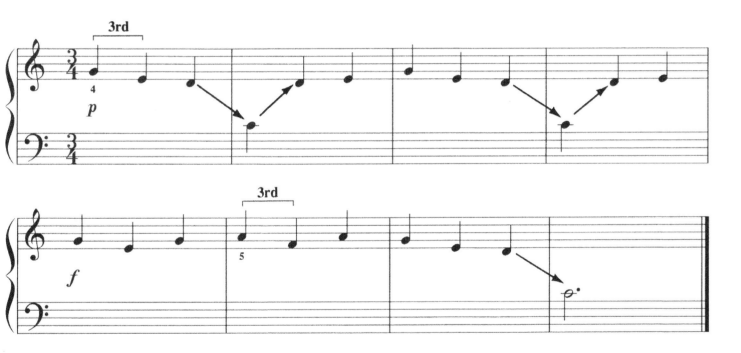

Edvard Grieg (GREEG) • 1843-1907 • Norway
Grieg was proud of his country, and his music consciously reflects his native folk music and culture. His works include orchestral suites, piano music and songs. His piano concerto is one of the most famous ever written.

Peer Gynt is the story of a young man with wild ideas and reckless actions. He travels throughout the world experiencing a series of weird adventures including romances with several women. Eventually he returns home to die in the arms of a girl he once abducted. *Morning* musically describes the sunrise as Peer Gynt views the world before him.

Schaum's **Fingerpower®, Primer Level** provides basic technic exercises to strengthen fingers and develop dexterity.

Intervals of a 4th and 5th

The *interval number* is the same as the number of *alphabet letters* that it includes. (See page 12). It is also the same as the number of white keys involved.

A up to D is a *4th*, because the distance in sound is 4 alphabet letters (A-B-C-D).
G up to C is also a *4th*, because the distance is again 4 alphabet letters (G-A-B-C).

D *down* to G is a *5th*, because the distance in sound is 5 alphabet letters (D-C-B-A-G).
C *down* to F is also a *5th*, because the distance is again 5 alphabet letters (C-B-A-G-F).

Intervals between other letters are counted the same way.

For intervals moving up, the alphabet goes *forward*. Brackets show sample **4ths** in the measure below.

For intervals moving *down*, the alphabet goes *backward*. Brackets show sample **5ths** in the measure below.

Artist's Life Waltz (Strauss)

Directions: This piece uses intervals of 4ths and 5ths, up and down. Try to recognize the 4ths and 5ths *with your eyes* as you play. Watch for a change of hand position, with thumb on D, in the second line of music. Arrows are used to show where hands alternate. If helpful, add brackets to show the 4th and 5ths, as in the sample above.

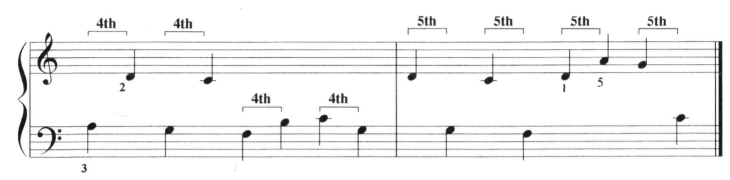

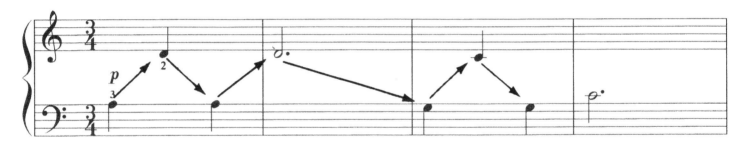

Johann Strauss, Jr. (STROWS) • 1825-1899 • Austria
Strauss was known as the "Waltz King" because he wrote about 400 waltzes during his lifetime. His father and brothers, Josef and Eduard, were also composers of waltzes and all conducted their own dance orchestras. The **waltz**, a dance in 3/4 time, was new at the time, extremely popular and considered avant garde and somewhat daring, because the couples held each other while dancing. Elaborate ballrooms were frequently crowded with patrons.

Like many of Strauss' waltzes, Artist's Life is quite lengthy - a collection of several sections, each with two or more themes. This is one of nine themes united under the same title.

Dotted Half Notes in 4/4 Time

A dotted half note is combined with a quarter note to make four counts in one measure, as shown below.
The counting numbers are printed between the staffs.

She Wore A Yellow Ribbon (American Folk Song)

Directions: As a preparatory, count and clap the rhythm for the entire piece. Be sure to keep hands together for the full three beats of each dotted half note. For ear training and vocal development, sing along as you practice.

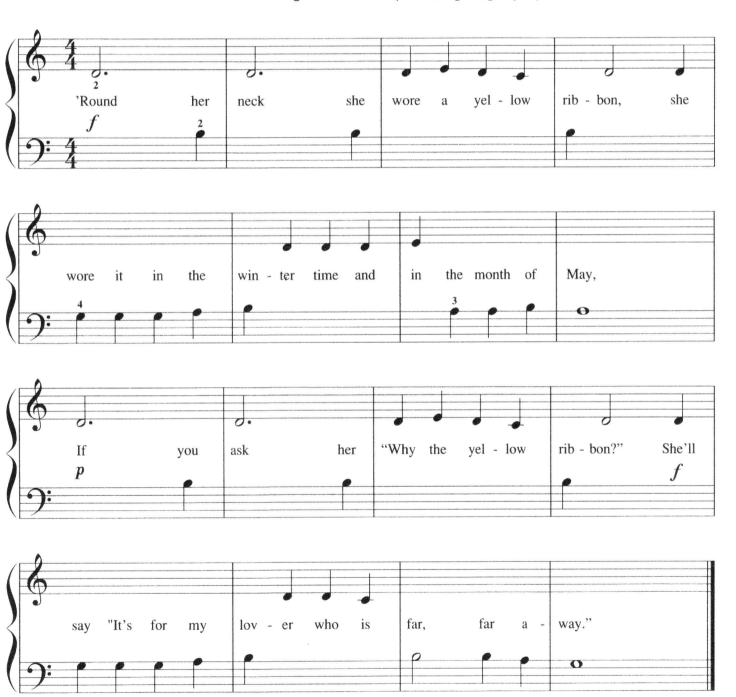

20

Pick-Up or Up-Beat Note

The note at the beginning of this piece, alone in an incomplete measure, is called a "pick-up" or "up-beat" note. The counts missing at the beginning of this piece are blaanced by the final measure. The first and last measures, when combined, add up to four beats.

Sharp Sign

The symbol # is called a **sharp** sign.
It is always positioned to the *left* of the note.
It means to go UP (to the right) to the nearest key.

C# is a black key, shown in the diagram.

F#, also a black key, is used on page 21.

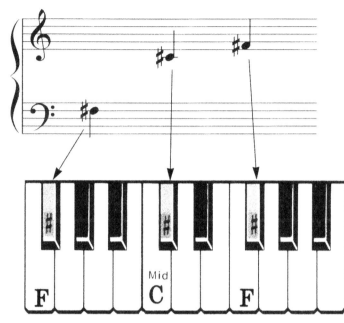

Allegro (Mozart, K3)

Directions: As a preparatory, count and clap the rhythm to this piece. Sample counting numbers are printed between the staffs. Be careful of the counting in the first and last measures. Notice the special fingering used for the black key.

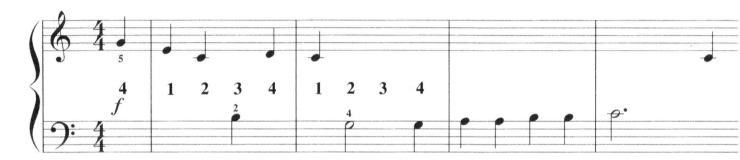

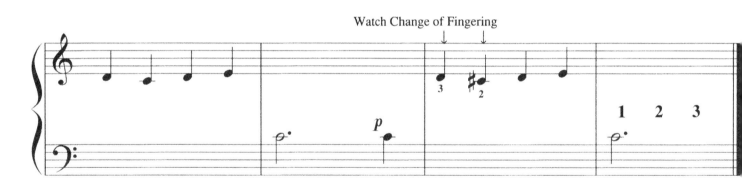

Wolfgang Amadeus Mozart (MOE-tsart) • 1756-1791 • Austria
Because of the quality of his music and the ease and speed with which he wrote, Mozart is considered a musical genius. He began lessons with his father at age 3 and wrote his first music at age 5. This piece is one of his early compositions, numbered K3, meaning the 3rd piece he wrote. In some cases the K-number is for a *group* of pieces, as on page 21. K stands for Kochel (KESH-ell), the man who cataloged Mozart's music. The title word, **Allegro** (ah-LEG-grow), means *fast* or *quick* in Italian.

Mozart lived only 35 years, but composed an enormous amount of music including operas, oratorios, symphonies and church music. His works are famous all over the world.

Duet Accompaniment

A **duet** is music for two performers. At the piano, a duet means two players sitting side-by-side. Sometimes, the term *one-piano four-hands* is used to describe this kind of duet.

In Mozart's time, duets were very unusual. He and his sister, Nannerl, caused great excitement in audiences when they performed duets as children.

German Dance (Mozart, K6000, No.6)

Directions: As a preparatory, count and clap the rhythm to this piece. Watch for the "pick-up" note at the beginning. Counting numbers are printed between the staffs. This piece uses F# several times (see page 20). Be careful of the correct fingering, especially in left hand. The duet accompaniment is intended for the teacher or advanced student. Learn to play the solo part comfortably before adding the duet.

Watch Finger Change.

DUET ACCOMPANIMENT

Rests

A rest is a musical symbol for silence. It shows places where *nothing* is to sound. Rests are named and counted the same as notes.

The whole rest and half rest look almost alike. Both rests are between the same two staff lines.

The *whole* rest is *below* the staff line.

The *half* rest is *above* the staff line.

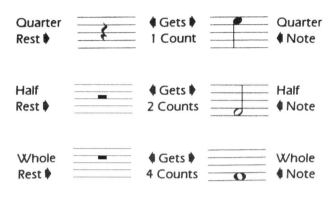

Quarter Rest ♦	♦ Gets ♦ 1 Count	Quarter ♦ Note
Half Rest ♦	♦ Gets ♦ 2 Counts	Half ♦ Note
Whole Rest ♦	♦ Gets ♦ 4 Counts	Whole ♦ Note

Flat Sign

The symbol ♭ is called a flat sign. It is always positioned to the *left* of the note. It means to go DOWN (to the left) to the nearest key. E-flat and B-flat are black keys, as shown below.

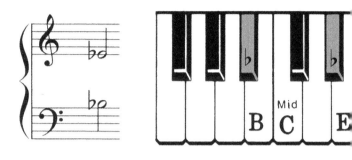

Use of the Flat Sign

A flat sign affects all other notes in the same measure that are on the *same line or space*. In measure 6 of the piece below, this means that both B's are to be made flat, even though the flat sign is used only with the first note. The same is true of the sharp sign.

The Stars Were Shining from "Tosca" (Puccini)

Directions: In the first measure, *nothing* sounds on the first beat (both hands have a rest). This also occurs in measures 5 and 7. As a preparatory, count and clap the *treble clef* rhythm for this piece. Clap only for the notes, do *not* clap for any rests. For extra practice, count and clap the *bass clef* rhythm for this piece. The counting numbers are printed between the staffs. If necessary, write in the counting for the second line of music.

Be sure this note is also FLAT.

Giacomo Puccini (poo-CHEE-nee) • 1858-1924 • Italy
Puccini is famous for his many operas of which *La Boheme*, *Tosca*, and *Madame Butterfly* are the best known. An **opera** (AH-per-ah) is a musical drama with emphasis on singing of vocal solos, ensembles and choruses with orchestral accompaniment. Staging includes a full array of costumes, props, scenery, lighting and special effects.

This theme is taken from Act III of "Tosca," a story of romance, political intrigue, revenge and remorse.

Whole Rest = Whole Measure

A *whole* rest is commonly used to fill a *whole measure* regardless of the number of counts indicated by the time signature. In this piece, the whole rest gets three counts because the time signature is 3/4.

Whole Rest

Waltz (Schubert, Op.127, No.5)

Directions: As a preparatory, count and clap the *treble clef* rhythm for this piece. Clap only for the notes, do *not* clap for any rests. For extra practice, count and clap the *bass clef* rhythm for this piece. This piece has a "pick up" note at the beginning (see page 20). Watch the finger numbers carefully, especially for the black keys.

DUET ACCOMPANIMENT

Franz Schubert (SHOO-burt) • 1797-1828 • Austria

Schubert was a very prolific composer, sometimes writing six to eight songs in one day. By age 23 he had written more than 500 works including operas, symphonies, chamber music, religious music and vocal music.

Op. is the abbreviation of the Latin word, **opus** (OH-puss), which is a unit of musical work numbered in chronological order. It is a composition of any length from a short single piece to a full symphony. This waltz is the 5th of a set of 20, written in 1815.

Playing Hands Together

Notes in the treble and bass staffs, placed directly above one another, are to be played at the same time. It will take a little time t
develop the coordination needed to play hands together accurately.

When playing hands together be careful that both notes sound simultaneously. In this piece, all the bass clef notes are whole note
Be sure to hold the key down for the full duration of four counts.

Rests should be observed by holding the hand and fingers slightly above the keys for the duration of each rest. The hand should b
kept in position, ready to play the next note following the rest.

Lightly Row   (German Folk Song)

Directions: As a preparatory, count and clap the *treble clef* rhythm for this piece. Sample counting numbers are shown between t
staffs. Clap only for the notes, do *not* clap for any rests. For extra practice, count and clap the *bass clef* rhythm for this piece.

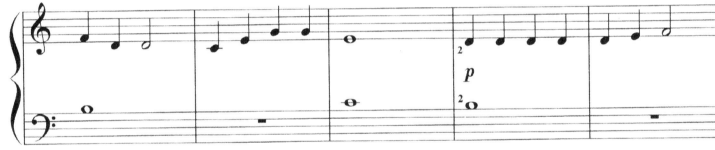

DUET ACCOMPANIMENT

Key Signature: G Major

A *key signature* is at the beginning of each staff, next to the clef sign. One or more sharps can be used in the key signature. (One or more flats may also be used.)

One sharp is the key signature for the *Key of G Major*. It means that <u>every F in both staffs is sharp</u>.

A key signature eliminates the need to write an individual sharp sign for every F.

Sweet Betsy from Pike (American Folk Song)

Directions: Be sure to play all F's sharp as indicated in the key signature.
Watch the finger numbers carefully, especially for the black keys.

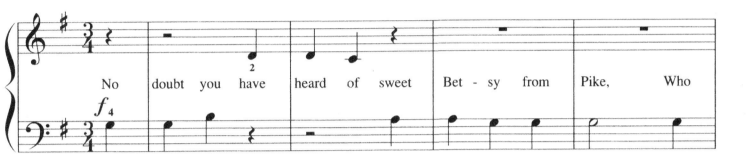

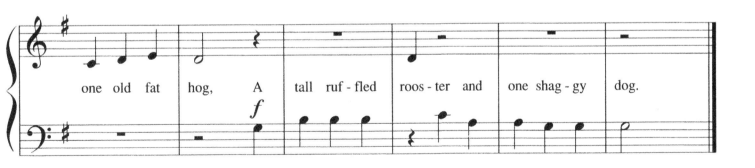

DUET ACCOMPANIMENT

Interval of a 6th

The 6ths shown in the sample to the right are used in the piece below.

E to G is a 6th because is spans 6 alphabet letters (E-D-C-B-A-G).

C to A is also a 6th (C-D-E-F-G-A).

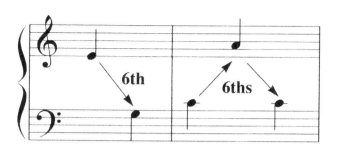

Pas de Deux from "Giselle" (Adam)

Directions: As a preparatory, count and clap the *treble clef* rhythm for this piece. Clap only for the notes, do *not* clap for any rests. For extra practice, count and clap the *bass clef* rhythm for this piece. Arrows are used to point out two of the 6th intervals. Try finding the other 6ths. Be aware of the starting finger and different hand position for the right hand.

Adolphe Adam (ah-DAHM) • 1803-1856 • France

Adam was a composer of comic operas and ballets which were internationally famous in their day. He wrote 15 ballets, 70 operas, plus sacred music, vocal and choral pieces.

A **ballet** (bal-LAY) is a theatrical performance by a dancing group usually telling a story or depicting a mood; the dancing pantomimes the story. *Giselle* is a story of love between a nobleman and a peasant girl. Disguise, deceit and ghostly intervention leave both of them dead. A **pas de deux** (pah deh DUH) is a French name for a dance by two persons.

2/4 Time Signature

2 — TWO *counts* or *beats* in each measure (see page 6).

4 — QUARTER note gets ONE count.

Preparatory: Count and clap the rhythm to the notes below. The counting numbers are printed between the staffs. Keep your counting very steady and even.

Theme from 5th Symphony (Beethoven, Op.67)

Directions: If helpful, add *counting numbers* to the remainder of the music.

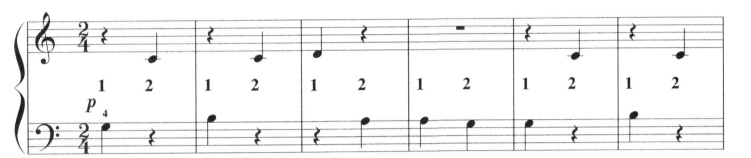

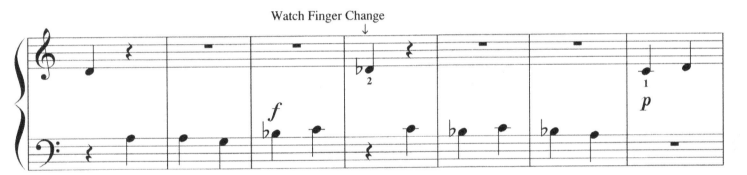

Watch Finger Change

Ludwig Van Beethoven (BAY-toe-ven) • 1770-1827 • Germany

As a child, Beethoven studied with both Mozart and Haydn. When Beethoven was 30 years old he started to become deaf. He continued to compose, however, and some of his most wonderful music was written after he had completely lost his hearing. Beethoven is recognized world-wide as one of the greatest composers of all time.

A **symphony** is a lengthy work for orchestra. The music is divided into contrasting sections called **movements**. Each movement has several themes. Beethoven is most famous for his nine symphonies of which the 5th is probably the best known. This theme is from the first movement.

28

Eighth Notes

When the *stems* of two quarter notes are joined by a heavy line called a **beam**, they become **eighth notes**. Eighth notes are played *twice as fast* as quarter notes. Eighth note counting is shown for these sample measures.

1 2 + 3 4   1 2 + 3 4 +

*Preparatory: Count and clap the rhythm to the measures above. The counting is printed below the notes. Keep your counting especially steady and even. Be careful to differentiate between the quarter notes and eighth notes.

Theme from First Symphony (Brahms, Op.68)

Directions: As a preparatory, count and clap the treble clef rhythm for this piece. Clap only for the notes, do not clap for any rests. Sample counting numbers are printed below the notes. If necessary, write in counting for the remainder of the piece. Watch for the changes of fingering in the last line.

Watch Finger Number Changes

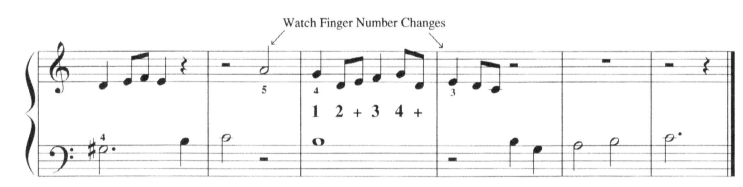

Johannes Brahms • 1833-1897 • Germany

Brahms was famous as a composer and pianist. He started his piano study at age 7 and by age 14 gave this first public recital which included one of his own compositions. Although he lived in poverty as a child, he prospered from his performances and music sales.

His music is of consistently high quality because he was fussy about his writing and often revised and refined the music many times before he would permit it to be published.

Brahms wrote four symphonies, chamber music, overtures, piano and vocal music. It took him many years to complete his first symphony. This theme is from the fourth movement.

*Teachers Note: The student should say the word "and" where a plus sign (+) is written. Other abbreviations of "and" may be used, if desired.

New Notes: Bass D and E – Leger Line B

Refer to the keyboard diagram on the front inside cover to locate the position of the two new bass notes at the end of this piece.

A **leger line** is a short extra line used to extend the staff up or down. Middle-C is written on a leger line. In this piece, the right hand plays the leger line note B, below middle C.

Iroquois Harvest Festival (Native American)

Directions: As a preparatory, count and clap the rhythm for the notes of this piece. Sample counting numbers are printed between the staffs. If necessary, write in the counting for the remainder of the piece.

Notice the new hand position in *both hands*. This is needed because of the new bass notes, D and E, at the end of the last line of music, and to enable the right hand to play the new leger line note, B, below middle-C.

Native American Music

Like most folk music, American Indian music evolved as it was passed on by memory from one generation to another. This melody is an authentic Iroquois tribal theme collected and transcribed by Harvey Worthington Loomis.

Key Signature: F Major
One *flat* is the key signature for the *Key of F Major.* It means that <u>all B's on the keyboard are flat</u>. A key signature eliminates the need to write an individual flat sign for every B.

Tempo Mark
Tempo is the rate of speed for a piece of music. The *tempo mark* is usually an Italian word (or several words) placed at the beginning of a piece. Look up the word, *Andante*, in the Music Dictionary on page 47.

Pilgrim's Chorus from "Tannhauser" (Wagner)
Directions: Be sure to play all B's flat as indicated in the key signature.
Watch the finger numbers carefully, especially for the black keys.

DUET ACCOMPANIMENT

Richard Wagner (VAHG-ner) • 1813-1883 • Germany
Wagner became profoundly interested in composing after hearing Beethoven's symphonies (see page 27). Wagner is remembered primarily for his operas, the best known of which involved stories of German mythology.

"Tannhauser" was one of his early operas, first performed in 1845. It is a story of love involving a singing contest where Tannhauser, a knight, is condemned by his colleagues. Elisabeth, his lady love, dies of a broken heart not realizing Tannhauser had been forgiven and reconciled.

Interval of a 7th
In this piece an arrow points out the interval of a 7th.

Can Can from "La Vie Parisienne" (Offenbach)

Directions: This piece uses a 2/4 time signature (refer to page 27). As a preparatory, count and clap the rhythm to this piece. Sample counting numbers are printed between the staffs. Be sure to play all B's *flat* as indicated in the key signature.

DUET ACCOMPANIMENT

Jacques Offenbach (OFF-fen-bahk) • 1819-1880 • France (Germany)
Although born in Germany, Offenbach spent most of his life in France and is usually considered a French composer. He was a professional cello player and conductor in Paris. He is most famous for his comic operas and wrote 97 of them during his lifetime.

"La Vie Parisienne" reflects life in Paris during the 1860's. The **can-can** is a high-kicking dance considered naughty and daring in its day because women flounced their skirts revealing their legs.

New Note: Bass C
The sample staff at the right shows the new bass note, C, along with left hand finger numbers for a new hand position.

Broken Chords
A **chord** is a group of three or more notes sounded at the same time. A **broken chord** separates the notes of a chord, as found in the last measure of the 1st, 2nd and 3rd lines of music below.

Chords are formed by combining intervals, as shown in the "Broken Chord Etude" below.

An **etude** is a muscial exercise for the fingers, like a calisthenic.

Broken Chord Etude (Schaum)

Directions: The first line of music shows how two intervals of a 3rd are combined to form a C chord. Interval numbers are printed above the notes. The second line uses the interval of a 3rd plus a 2nd to form a G7 chord. Notice that the two notes of a 2nd, when sharing the same stem, form a unique cluster. It is important that you train your eyes to recognize this interval of a 2nd.

Notice the new hand position indicated by finger numbers in the left hand. The third and fourth lines of music combine the same intervals to form C and G7 chords in the treble staff. See page 33 for an explanation of chord symbols.

Chord Symbols

A *chord symbol* is a kind of musical shorthand to identify various chords. It consists of a combination of letters, numbers and other symbols, placed directly above where the chord is to begin. Each broken chord on this page is identified with its chord symbol.

Notice the groups of finger numbers in the samples, one for each note of the broken chords. This left hand fingering is to be used in both pieces on this page.

Skip To My Lou (American Folk Song)

Directions: As a preparatory, play the entire piece several times, hands separately. When playing hands together, be careful to play the left hand notes precisely with the right hand notes.

Aunt Rhody (American Folk Song)

Directions: As a preparatory, play the entire piece, hands separately. The words for a song are sometimes called **lyrics**. In the 4th measure of the first line of music, notice that two 8th notes fit with one syllable. For vocal development and additional coordination, try singing while you play.

Natural Sign – Accidentals

A natural sign cancels a sharp or flat until the next measure bar line. A natural is always a white key.

An **accidental** is the name given to a sharp, flat or natural sign used separately from a key signature. An accidental <u>affects all notes of the same pitch</u> for the remainder of the measure. A measure bar cancels an accidental.

♮ — **natural**

♭ — **flat**

♯ — **sharp**

Danse Macabre (Saint-Saens)

Directions: This piece contains many accidentals. Watch the finger numbers carefully, especially for the black keys. The natural sign is used here to cancel the flat in the key signature. The flat sign is used as a reminder to restore the key signature.

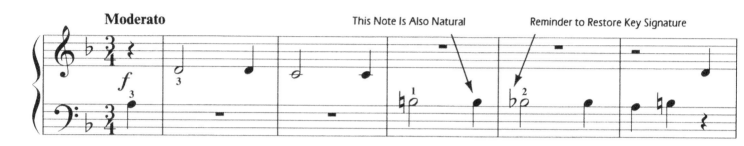

DUET ACCOMPANIMENT

Camille Saint-Saens (sann-SAWN) • 1835-1921 • France
Saint-Saens was a very gifted child who gave a formal debut recital at age 10, by which time he had memorized all 32 of Beethoven's piano sonatas (over 650 pages of difficult music). After graduating from the Paris Conservatory, he became famous as a virtuoso organist and master of improvisation. He made a very successful tour of the United States in 1915.

"Danse Macabre," written in 1874, is an orchestral work called a symphonic poem. It depicts a ghostly, spooky mood.

The Tie

The *tie* is a curved line that connects two notes on the *same line or space* that are *next to each other* (even if there is a bar line in between). A tie may be used in the treble staff or bass staff.

The duration of the tied notes is *added together* joining into one continuous sound, therefore, the *second* note is *not* played. A tie adds to the duration of the first note, but does not change the counting.

Depending upon the direction of the stems, the tie may be above or below the note heads, as shown in this sample.

Down in the Valley (American Folk Song)

Directions: Notice the change of right hand fingering for the note, B, at the beginning of the second line of music. Use the chord fingering shown on page 33. The final measure has a blocked chord where *three notes are played simultaneously*. Use fingers 1-3-5 to play this blocked chord.

New Notes: Treble B and C
The sample staff at the right shows two new treble notes, B and C, with right hand finger numbers for a new hand position.

The Octave
Octave is the name given to the interval of an 8th. The lower and upper notes of an octave have the *same letter name*. The octave is pointed out with arrows.

Come To the Sea (Italian Folk Song)

Directions: Notice the change of right hand fingering for the new note, C, at the end of the first line of music. The hand position changes again in the third measure of the last line of music. A wide stretch of the right hand is needed to play the octave, pointed out by an arrow. Can you find another octave in this piece?

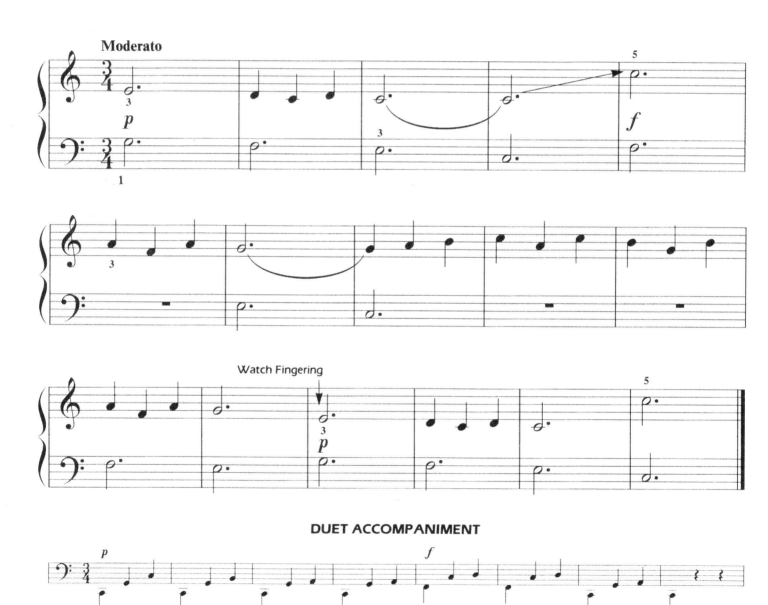

Dissonance

A *dissonance* is a combination of simultaneous music sounds that seem harsh or unpleasant to the listener. It is often used to create dramatic effects: feelings of tension, unrest or conflict.

The interval of a 7th is the dissonance shown here with arrows. Notice how the dissonance on the first count is resolved on the third count in each of these measures.

Theme from Symphony No. 6 (Tchaikowsky, Op.74)

Directions: This piece has many changes of fingering for the right hand. Watch the finger numbers closely. Be careful of the rhythm in measures with counting numbers. Dissonant 7ths are shown with arrows. Can you find the interval of an octave in the melody?

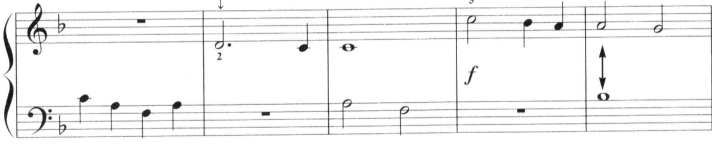

Peter I. Tchaikowsky (chy-CUFF-skee) • 1840-1893 • Russia

Tchaikowsky is considered one of Russia's greatest composers. His ballets, symphonies, and concertos are frequently performed throughout the world. His music has great contrasts in mood ranging from intensity to tenderness. He was professor of harmony at the Moscow Conservatory and well known as a conductor. He visited the United States in 1891 where he was a guest conductor at the opening of Carnegie Hall in New York City.

Tchaikowsky's sixth and last symphony was written in 1893. It is nicknamed the "Pathetique" because of its melancholy mood.

Transposing

To *transpose* means to play in a different key. This involves changing the key signature. In the music below, the same theme appears in the key of G major, and in the key of C major. In these two versions, the fingering, counting and intervals remain the same, only the notes change.

Key of G major: **The Bear Went Over the Mountain** (American Folk Song)

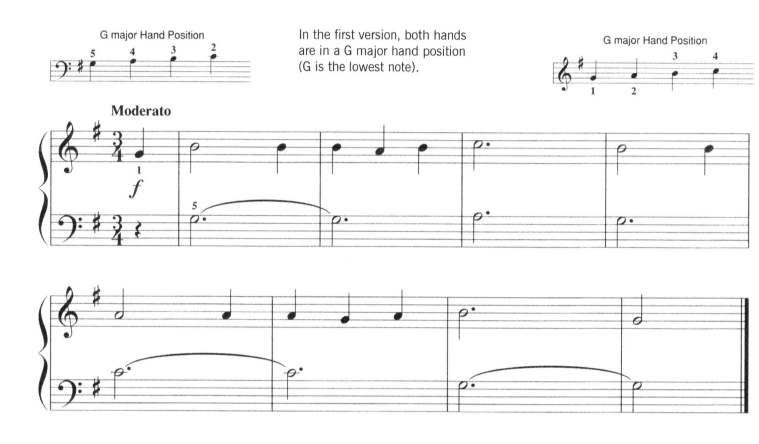

In the first version, both hands are in a G major hand position (G is the lowest note).

Key of C major: **The Bear Went Over the Mountain** (American Folk Song)

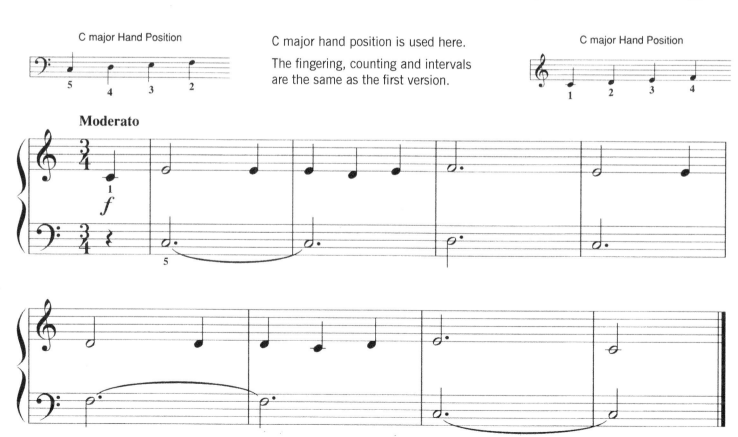

C major hand position is used here.

The fingering, counting and intervals are the same as the first version.

More Transposing

In the music below, the same theme appears in the key of C major and in the key of F major.
In the first version, both hands are in a C major hand position (C is the lowest note).
In the second version, an F major hand position is used.

Key of C major: **Jingle Bells** (Pierpont)

Key of F major: **Jingle Bells** (Pierpont)

One flat in the key signature means all B's are flat.

F Chord

The F chord pattern, along with the C and G chords, is shown here with the left hand fingering for each chord.

Fewer **chord symbols** are used in this piece. Instead of repeating the same chord symbol, measure after measure, it is now assumed that the same chord continues until a new chord symbol is used. Therefore, the C chord, which appears in the second measure, is also to be used in the next five measures. Chord symbols will be used in this way from now on.

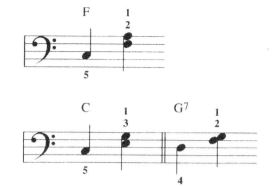

When the Saints Go Marching In (American Folk Song)

Directions: The tie at the end of the first line of music is continued to the first measure of the next line.

Similar ties occur later on this page. Notice that the left hand chords have various rhythms, although the notes remain the same for each chord.

Staccato

A dot, *directly above or below* a note head means to play with a short, quick release, as though you were touching something hot. This is called *staccato*.

A staccato note is shorter than normal, but NOT faster.

Staccato notes are shown in the sample.

Las Chiapanecas (Mexican Folk Song)

Directions: This piece has many staccato notes which are to be played in a detached, separated manner. In contrast, the dotted-half notes are to be sustained and held for their full value.

This piece is sometimes called the "Mexican Clap-Hands Dance."

DUET ACCOMPANIMENT

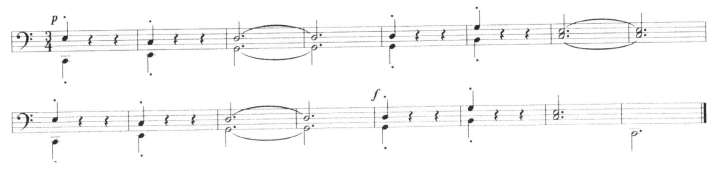

Four 8th Notes Beamed Together

Two or more 8th notes may share the same beam. They are counted the same as other 8th notes (see page 28). The samples here have the counting printed between the staffs.

Melody and Accompaniment

This piece has several measures where the interval of a 3rd is used as an accompaniment. These accompaniment notes must be played softly. They are marked with the symbol *p* meaning soft (see page 14).

Lavender's Blue   (English Folk Song)

Directions: As a preparatory, count and clap the melody notes for the first four measures. This same 4-measure rhythm pattern is repeated three more times in the remainder of the piece. If helpful, write in the counting numbers for the first four measures.

This piece has one sharp in the key signature (see page 25). Be sure to play *all F's sharp*.
Watch for the change of fingering on the F-sharp for left hand, near the end.

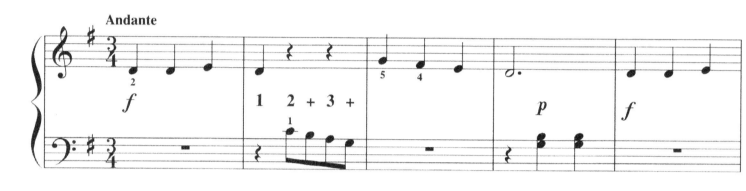

DUET ACCOMPANIMENT

Musette (Bach)

Directions: As a preparatory, count and clap the melody notes for the first eight measures. This same 8-measure rhythm pattern is repeated once more in the remainder of the piece. Counting numbers are printed between the staffs. See page 27 for a review of the 2/4 time signature. Watch for the staccato notes (see page 41).

The left hand plays an *accompaniment* throughout this piece. Be sure to play this accompaniment softer so the right hand melody can be heard clearly.

DUET ACCOMPANIMENT

A **musette** (mew-ZETT) is an instrument like a bagpipe, used in music of the 1700's. The instrument pictured here is a bagpipe. The low bass notes in the duet accompaniment imitate the drone bass of the musette.

For information about the composer, Bach, see page 16.

Bagpipe

Major and Minor

A melody in a major key usually sounds happy, cheerful and bright. In a minor key, the same melody sounds sad, mysterious and spooky. This page has two versions of the melody "Alouette."

Major Key Version: **Alouette** (French Folk Song)

Directions: This piece has a G major key signature (see page 25).

Minor Key Version: **Alouette** (French Folk Song)

Directions: This piece has several accidental flats (see page 34). Notice the minor sound which contrasts to the major in the piece above. Watch for use of the right hand thumb at the end of the first line.

Teacher's Note: The purpose of this lesson is to acquaint the student with the *sound* of major and minor, therefore, accidentals are used for the minor version. A technical explanation of major and parallel minor will be presented at a more advanced level.

Multiple Tied Notes

The left hand has several intervals of a 3rd where both notes are tied into the next measure. Each tied note has its own tie. Notice the position of the two curved lines for these tied notes in the bass staff. The two measures at the end of the piece also have a tied note in the right hand.

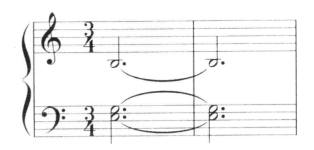

On With the Show from "Pagliacci" (Leoncavallo)

Directions: This piece is in a minor key and has several accidental sharps.

Watch for fingering changes in both hands, shown with arrows.

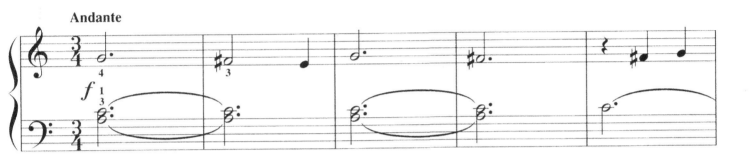

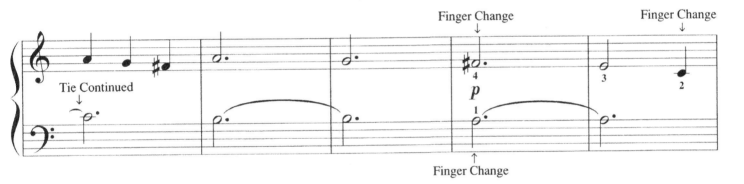

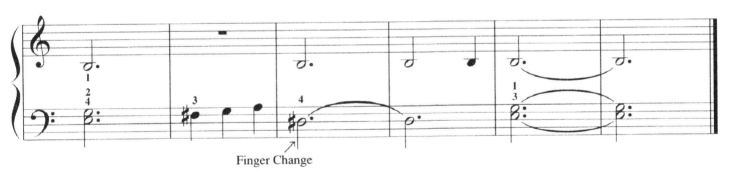

Ruggiero Leoncavallo (lay-on-kay-VAL-loh) • 1857-1919 • Italy

Leoncavallo was a composer and pianist. As a young man he earned a living playing piano in cafes throughout Europe. Although he wrote songs, piano solos, choral music and eleven other operas, he is remembered mainly for the opera, *Pagliacci*, which was first performed in 1892.

The story of *Pagliacci* is a love triangle which ends in tragedy. This melody, in a minor key, is sung by an actor portraying a clown, who is inwardly saddened with anger and grief over his wife's infidelity.

Review

This piece includes many things presented previously in this book, such as accidentals, 8th notes, the tie, chord symbols, melody and accompaniment. If you have any questions, use the music dictionary on page 47 or the index on page 48.

It is a good idea to review some of the other pieces in this book. Try to play them with improved accuracy using the proper tempo and observing the dynamic marks. Also try playing several favorite pieces from memory (without using the music).

Blues Ending (Schaum)

Directions: As a preparatory, count and clap the treble staff notes for the first four measures. This same 4-measure rhythm pattern is repeated in the second line of music. Counting numbers are printed between the staffs. Then count and clap the treble staff notes in the third line of music. If helpful, write the counting numbers for the third line of music. At first, practice right hand alone until the rhythm is secure.

The sequence of chords used here is called a *blues progression*. It is used in various styles of music including blues, boogie and jazz. The **blues** is a slow, wistful style of music with jazz-type rhythms, originating with African-Americans during the early 1900's.

You are now ready to progress to *Schaum's Piano for Adults, Level One.*

MUSIC DICTIONARY

cent (ACK-sent) Stress or emphasis on a note or chord.

cidental (ack-sih-DEN-tal) Sharp, flat, or natural that does ot appear in the key signature. See page 34.

legro (ah-LEG-grow) Fast, quickly.

ndante (ahn-DAHN-tay) Moderately slow.

eam Thick line connecting the stems of two or more 8th otes. See page 28.

hord (KORD) Simultaneous sounding of three or more ones. See page 32.

resc. Abbreviation of *crescendo*.

rescendo (cre-SHEN-doh) Gradually increasing in loud-ess. Also abbreviated with the sign: —

im. Abbreviation of *diminuendo*.

iminuendo (di-min-you-END-oh) Becoming gradually less ud. Also abbreviated with the sign: —

issonance (DISS-uh-nunce) Combination of simultaneous usical sounds that are unpleasant or harsh to the listener. See age 37.

uet (doo-WHET) Music for two performers. See page 21.

ynamic marks Same as *expression marks*.

xpression marks Signs used to show different levels of loud nd soft. For example, *f* and *p*. See page 14.

f Abbreviation of *forte*: loud.

ff Abbreviation of *fortissimo*: very loud.

forte (FOHR-tay) Loud, strong. Abbreviation: *f*

fortissimo (fohr-TISS-ee-moh) Very loud. Abbreviation: *ff*

interval Distance in sound between one note and another. See pages 12 & 18.

key signature One or more sharps or flats at the beginning of each staff, next to the clef.

largo (LAHR-goh) Very slow, solemn.

legato (lah-GAH-toh) Notes played in a smooth and connected manner.

leger line (LED-jer) Short horizontal line placed above or below as an extension to the musical staff. Used for writing of individual notes beyond the normal range of the staff. Middle C is written on a leger line.

L.H. Abbreviation of *left hand*.

lento (LEN-toh) Slow, but not as slow as *largo*.

M.M. Abbreviation of Maelzel's metronome. See *metronome*.

metronome (MET-roh-nome) Device to determine tempo or speed in music. Measured in beats per minute. The original mechanical metronome was popularized by J.N. Maelzel, there-fore the abbreviation, M.M. (Maelzel's metronome).

minor Chord, melody, or scale often having a sad, mysterious, or spooky sound.

moderato (mah-dur-AH-toh) At a moderate tempo or speed.

note head Round part of a musical note.

octave (AHK-tiv) Interval of an 8th; the top and bottom notes have the same letter name.

op. Abbreviation of *opus*.

opus (OH-puss) Unit of musical work usually numbered in chronological order. May be a composition of any length from a short single piece to a full symphony.

p Abbreviation of *piano*: Soft.

pianissimo (pee-ah-NISS-ee-moh) Very soft. Abbreviation: *pp*

piano (pee-YAA-noh) Soft. Abbreviation: *p*

pianoforte (pee-yaa-noh-FOR-tay) Original full name for the *piano*, chosen because it was the first keyboard instrument to effectively play in a wide range of loudness; thus the combination of words *piano* and *forte* (literally: soft-loud). See page 4.

pp Abbreviation of *pianissimo*: Very soft.

repertoire (reh-per-TWAR) Musical compositions previously studied, mastered, and currently maintained by a musician or musical group so that performance can be given with a minimum of preparation.

rest A symbol for silence placed in the staff. A rest shows where and how long NO note is to sound. See page 22.

R.H. Abbreviation of *right hand*.

rit. Abbreviation of *ritardando*.

ritard. Abbreviation of *ritardando*.

ritardando (ree-tahr-DAHN-doh) Gradually getting slower in speed.

skip Movement from one musical letter to another, skipping one or more letters in between.

staccato (stah-KAH-toh) Short, detached, separated. Indicat-ed by a dot *above or below* a note head. See page 41.

staff 1) Group of five horizontal lines used for note place-ment. 2) System of two or more staffs joined by a brace or bracket. See page 9.

stem Vertical line attached to a note head.

step The distance from one musical letter to the very next letter.

tempo (TEMM-poh) Rate of speed used for musical beats or meter.

tempo mark Word or words at the beginning of a piece of music explaining the rate of speed to be used. For example, *allegro, andante, moderato*.

tie Curved line that connects two notes on the same line or space that are next to each other. The values of the tied notes are added together joining into one continuous sound. See page 35.

time signature Two large numbers, above each other in the staff, at the beginning of a piece of music. The *upper* number tells how many counting numbers or beats are in each mea-sure. The *lower* number tells which kind of note gets one counting number. If the lower number is 4, the *quarter note* gets one counting number. See page 13.

transpose (trans-POZE) To play a melody or chord in a differ-ent key, starting on a higher or lower note. When transposing, a different key signature and hand position are used. See page 38.

upbeat (UP-beet) One or more notes at the beginning of a piece, which are less than a complete measure. Often called *pick up notes*. See page 20.

Index